CROWNED WITH BEAUTY
Restored to Reign

A 12 WEEK GUIDE TO A HOLY GLOW RESET

MELISSA MENDEZ

CROWNED WITH BEAUTY - COPYRIGHT ® 2025 BY MELISSA MENDEZ

PUBLISHED BY UNITED HOUSE PUBLISHING

ALL RIGHTS RESERVED. NO PORTION OF THIS BOOK MAY BE REPRODUCED OR SHARED IN ANY FORM - ELECTRONIC, PRINTED, PHOTOCOPIED, RECORDING, OR BY ANY INFORMATION STORAGE OR RETRIEVAL SYSTEM, WITHOUT PRIOR WRITTEN PERMISSION FROM THE PUBLISHER. THE USE OF SHORT QUOTATIONS IS PERMITTED.

ALL SCRIPTURE QUOTATIONS, UNLESS OTHERWISE INDICATED, ARE TAKEN FROM THE HOLY BIBLE, NEW INTERNATIONAL VERSION®, NIV®. COPYRIGHT ©1973, 1978, 1984, 2011 BY BIBLICA, INC.TM USED BY PERMISSION OF ZONDERVAN. ALL RIGHTS RESERVED WORLDWIDE. WWW.ZONDERVAN.COMTHE "NIV" AND "NEW INTERNATIONAL VERSION" ARE TRADEMARKS REGISTERED IN THE UNITED STATES PATENT AND TRADEMARK OFFICE BY BIBLICA, INC.

SCRIPTURE TAKEN FROM THE NEW KING JAMES VERSION®. COPYRIGHT © 1982 BY THOMAS NELSON. USED BY PERMISSION. ALL RIGHTS RESERVED.

SCRIPTURE QUOTATIONS ARE FROM THE HOLY BIBLE, ENGLISH STANDARD VERSION® (ESV®), COPYRIGHT © 2001 BY CROSSWAY, A PUBLISHING MINISTRY OF GOOD NEWS PUBLISHERS. USED BY PERMISSION. ALL RIGHTS RESERVED.

ISBN:978-1-952840-79-1
UNITED HOUSE PUBLISHING CLARKSTON, MICHIGAN
INFO@UNITEDHOUSEPUBLISHING.COM WWW.UNITEDHOUSEPUBLISHING.COM

COVER & INTERIOR DESIGN: MELISSA MENDEZ

PRINTED IN THE UNITED STATES OF AMERICA 2025 - FIRST EDITION

SPECIAL SALES:
MOST UNITED HOUSE BOOKS ARE AVAILABLE AT SPECIAL QUANTITY DISCOUNTS WHEN PURCHASED IN BULK BY CORPORATIONS, ORGANIZATIONS, AND SPECIAL INTEREST GROUPS. FOR MORE INFORMATION,
PLEASE EMAIL ORDERS@ UNITEDHOUSEPUBLISHING.COM.

DEDICATION

TO MY BEAUTIFUL **MOM**, WHO TAUGHT ME THE POWER OF FAITH AND THE BEAUTY OF A WOMAN FULLY SURRENDERED TO GOD.

TO MY DAUGHTERS, **JOCELYN AND SOFIA,** AND MY SON, **ELIAS**—MY GREATEST TREASURES AND DAILY REMINDERS OF GOD'S GOODNESS. MAY YOU ALWAYS KNOW THAT YOUR WORTH AND IDENTITY ARE ROOTED IN JESUS.

TO MY SISTER, **DIANA**, THANK YOU FOR YOUR LOVE, SUPPORT, AND FOR ALWAYS BELIEVING IN THE CALLING GOD PLACED ON MY LIFE.

TO MY FRIENDS—**AMBER, BETH, DIANNE, ROXY, CARELI, EVA, MIRIAM, AND ROSEMARY**—MY PRAYER WARRIORS AND TRUE KINGDOM WOMEN. THANK YOU FOR STANDING IN THE GAP, LIFTING ME IN PRAYER, AND REMINDING ME OF GOD'S PROMISES WHEN I NEEDED THEM MOST.

TO EVERY WOMAN WHO WILL HOLD THIS DEVOTIONAL IN HER HANDS—MAY THESE PAGES SPEAK LIFE TO YOUR SOUL, DRAW YOU CLOSER TO JESUS, AND REMIND YOU THAT YOU ARE, INDEED, CROWNED WITH BEAUTY.

Y A MI AMA, GRACIAS POR ABRIRME CAMINO CON SUS ORACIONES Y POR CUBRIRNOS CON SU AMOR. ESTE LEGADO DE FE ES TAMBIÉN SUYO, LAS GENERACIONES QUE VINIERON ANTES DE USTED Y LAS QUE SIGUEN.

01 – WECOME & FOUNDATIONS

WELCOME LETTER...7
THE HOLY GLOW RESET...9
HOW TO USE THIS DEVOTIONAL (R.E.I.G.N. METHOD).........11
BRAND MISSION..15

02–WEEKLY DEVOTIONALS

WEEK 1: CHOSEN FOR ROYALTY..19
WEEK 2: THE PROCESS OF PREPARATION.................................27
WEEK 3: BEAUTY TREATMENTS & BECOMING..........................35
WEEK 4: FAVOR IN THE PALACE...43
WEEK 5: THE POWER OF IDENTITY...51
WEEK 6: COURAGE IN THE CALL..59
WEEK 7: STEPPING OUT IN FAITH..67
WEEK 8: APPROACHING THE KING..75
WEEK 9: STRATEGY AND DISCERNMENT...................................83
WEEK 10: EXPOSING THE ENEMY..91
WEEK 11: SEALED WITH AUTHORITY..99
WEEK 12: RESTORED TO REIGN...107

03– GET CONNECTED

ABOUT THE AUTHOR..113
THE COMMUNITY..115

WELCOME

Dear Royal Beauty,

Welcome to the Crowned with Beauty Devotional—a sacred space created just for you.

I want to be honest with you from the start: for a long time, I struggled with insecurities. I didn't feel beautiful, worthy, or even sure of my purpose. Life often felt overwhelming, heavy, and confusing. In those moments, I questioned if I was enough. If I mattered. If God really saw me.

But in the depths of that struggle, I began to seek God for understanding. Slowly, He invited me to embrace my royal beauty—to recognize what it truly means to be His daughter, crowned with purpose and loved far beyond what I had imagined. That invitation sparked a journey of healing that changed everything.

Self-care became sacred, necessary even—a way to honor not just my body but my soul and spirit. Learning to care for my whole being became an act of worship, a holy rhythm of restoration and grace.

This devotional along with the movement "Embracing Royal Beauty" was born out of that journey—a desire to remind you, beloved daughter of the King, that you were never meant to live dimmed down, disconnected, or discouraged. You were created to radiate. You were crowned not only with beauty but with purpose, authority, and divine favor.

As you journey through these weekly reflections, I invite you to make space for stillness, for deep soul care, and for holy encounters. Each page was prayerfully written to help you reconnect with your identity and renew your spirit. This was created to be used along with Embracing Royal Beauty skincare (link below to purchase) and to be done in community to build a sisterhood that creates a ripple effect that fulfills the great commission to go and make disciples.

Let this devotional be more than words on a page—let it be a mirror that reflects your worth, a balm that soothes your weary places, and a well where your spirit is refreshed by Living Water.

With love,
Melissa
Founder, Embracing Royal Beauty

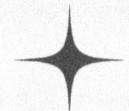

THE HOLY GLOW RESET

A 12-WEEK LIFESTYLE INTENTIONALLY DESIGNED TO HELP YOU LIVE IN ALIGNMENT WITH THE GREATEST COMMANDMENT: LOVE GOD, LOVE OTHERS, AND LOVE YOURSELF WELL.
IN A WORLD CONSTANTLY PULLING US IN A MILLION DIRECTIONS, THIS JOURNEY INVITES YOU TO PAUSE, SEEK GOD, AND REALIGN YOUR LIFE WITH HIS PURPOSE.
THE HOLY GLOW IS MORE THAN A SURFACE-LEVEL GLOW—IT'S A SACRED RADIANCE THAT FLOWS FROM A SOUL FULLY SURRENDERED AND A LIFE INTENTIONALLY LIVED.

HOLY MEANS SET APART.
THIS INVITATION ISN'T ABOUT HUSTLE OR PERFECTION. IT'S ABOUT CHOOSING A SLOWER, MORE SACRED PACE— ONE THAT REFLECTS GOD'S RHYTHM, NOT THE WORLD'S. THROUGH THIS JOURNEY, YOU'LL BEGIN FORMING RHYTHMS THAT NOURISH YOUR SPIRIT, SOUL, AND BODY —CREATING A GLOW THAT BEGINS IN HIS PRESENCE AND RADIATES OUTWARD.

DECLARATION: "I AM STEPPING INTO SACRED RHYTHMS. I AM GLOWING WITH HIS PRESENCE."

HOW TO USE THIS DEVOTIONAL:

AS AN ESTHETICIAN AND TRAUMA-INFORMED, SPIRIT-LED COACH, I SAW A GAP IN THE BEAUTY INDUSTRY—WHERE GLOW-UPS ARE OFTEN ONLY SKIN-DEEP AND FLEETING WITHOUT JESUS. MY OWN LIFE WAS TRANSFORMED THE MOMENT I LET HIM "EXFOLIATE" THE PAIN AND TRAUMA FROM MY SOUL AND POUR HIS LOVE INTO EVERY BROKEN PLACE. THAT LOVE THEN OVERFLOWED INTO MY RELATIONSHIPS, MY PURPOSE, AND EVEN THE WAY I CARE FOR MY SKIN.

THIS WEEKLY JOURNEY IS YOUR INVITATION TO R.E.I.G.N. IN YOUR GOD-GIVEN IDENTITY—AS A WOMAN CROWNED WITH BEAUTY AND CALLED WITH PURPOSE. THROUGH THE STORY OF QUEEN ESTHER, YOU'LL UNCOVER THE INTERNAL AND EXTERNAL PREPARATION THAT POSITIONED HER FOR ROYALTY.

EACH WEEK BLENDS SCRIPTURE, REFLECTION, AND INTENTIONAL SKINCARE—HELPING YOU SEE YOUR ROUTINE AS SACRED, NOT SUPERFICIAL. FOR A DEEPER EXPERIENCE, THE EMBRACING ROYAL BEAUTY LINE—CRAFTED WITH ORGANIC, WILD-CRAFTED, AND PRAYERFULLY ANOINTED INGREDIENTS—WAS CREATED TO SUPPORT YOU AS YOU RISE IN YOUR ROYAL IDENTITY. (LINKS TO PURCHASE IN THE BACK OF THE BOOK)

YOU WERE CREATED TO REIGN—WITH RADIANT GRACE, HOLY CONFIDENCE, AND DIVINE PURPOSE.

R.E.I.G.N

R – READ THE WORD

BEGIN BY READING THE WEEKLY SCRIPTURE SLOWLY AND PRAYERFULLY. LET IT WASH OVER YOU AND INVITE GOD TO SPEAK.

E – ENGAGE WITH THE DEVOTIONAL

READ THE WEEKLY MESSAGE AND REFLECT ON HOW IT SPEAKS TO YOUR CURRENT SEASON. LET THE HOLY SPIRIT HIGHLIGHT WHAT HE WANTS YOU TO RECEIVE.

I – INTEGRATE SOUL + SKIN CARE

PRACTICE THE SKINCARE RITUAL WITH INTENTION. USE THIS TIME AS SACRED—NURTURING YOUR BODY WHILE LETTING GOD CARE FOR YOUR SOUL.

G – GO DEEPER IN JOURNALING

USE THE JOURNAL PROMPTS TO EXPLORE YOUR THOUGHTS, EMOTIONS, AND INSIGHTS. WRITE FROM THE HEART. LET IT BE HONEST, HEALING, AND HOLY.

N – NOURISH IN PRAYER

CLOSE EACH WEEK IN PRAYER. SPEAK WITH GOD, LISTEN FOR HIS WHISPERS, AND BE REFRESHED IN HIS PRESENCE.

EMBRACING ROYAL BEAUTY: BRAND MISSION

At Embracing Royal Beauty, we believe every woman is born with a divine radiance—set apart, crowned with purpose, and created to reflect the glory of God.

Our mission is to help women rediscover their worth, restore their identity, and reign with confidence in every area of life.

We blend faith, holistic wellness, and intentional self-care to nurture the spirit, soul, and body. Through biblical truth, nourishing rituals, and community, we create sacred spaces where women feel seen, supported, and spiritually refreshed.

Whether it's through skincare, soul care, or scripture, our goal is to help women live from their royal identity—not just glowing on the outside, but thriving from the inside out.

You were made to shine. You were made to reign.

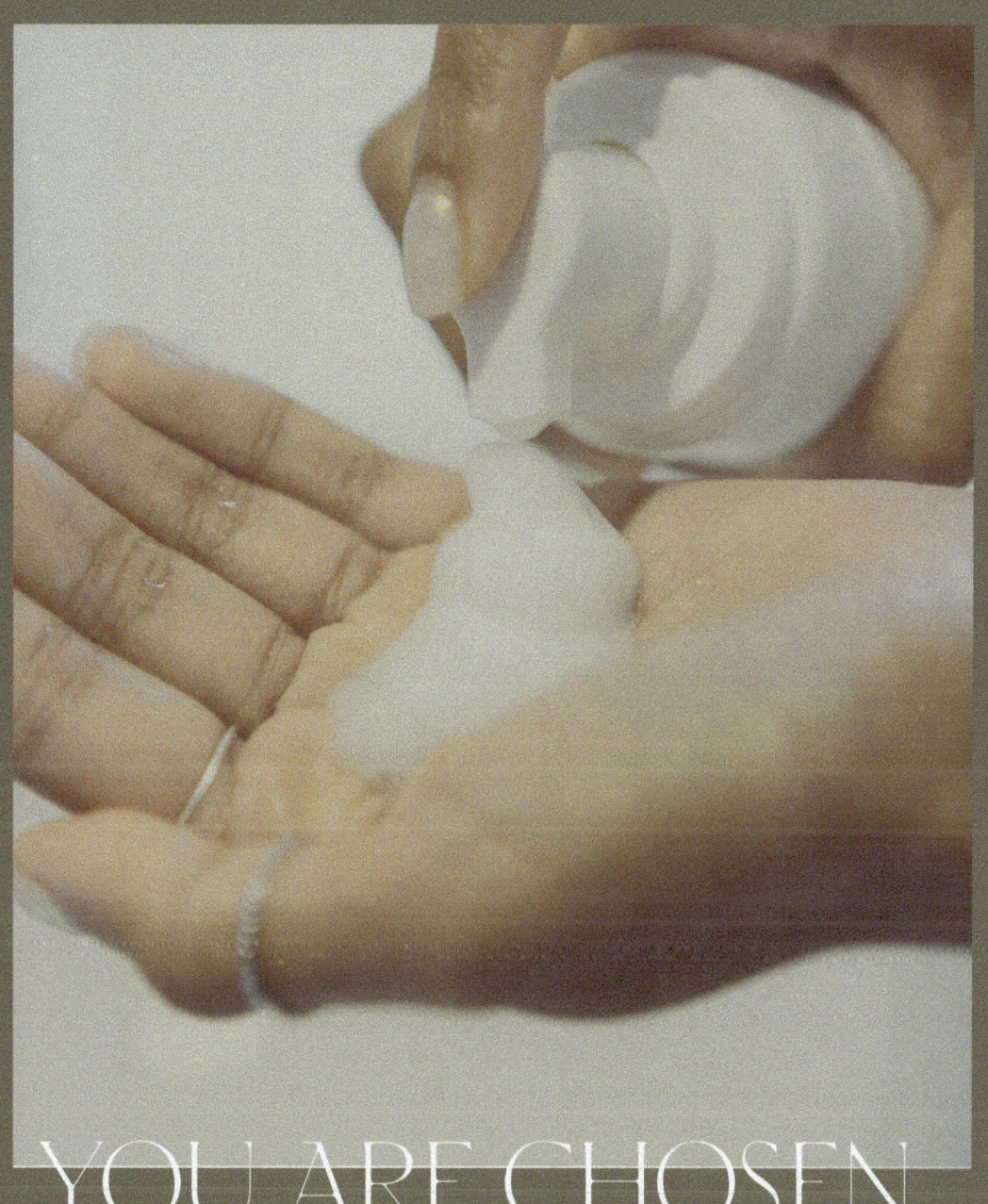

WEEK 1

CHOSEN FOR ROYALTY

THEME:
YOU ARE CHOSEN, EVEN IN THE HIDDEN PLACES.

SCRIPTURE:
"... THE YOUNG WOMAN WAS LOVELY AND BEAUTIFUL...
WHEN THE KING'S COMMAND AND DECREE WERE HEARD
... THAT ESTHER WAS ALSO TAKEN TO THE KING'S
PALACE, INTO THE CARE OF HEGAI THE CUSTODIAN OF
THE WOMEN..."
— ESTHER 2:7-9 (NKJV)

PRAYER:
FATHER, I THANK YOU FOR SEEING ME EVEN WHEN I FELT
HIDDEN. I THANK YOU FOR CHOOSING ME NOT ONLY AS YOUR
DAUGHTER BUT TO EXPAND YOUR KINGDOM. THANK YOU FOR
LEADING ME THROUGH THE PREPARATION WITH GRACE,
IN JESUS' NAME AMEN.

DEVOTIONAL REFLECTION:

Esther's story doesn't start with a crown—it begins in obscurity. She was an orphaned girl, quietly raised by her cousin Mordecai, with no royal lineage and no clue of the future ahead of her. And yet, she was seen. She was chosen. She was brought in.

When I first felt called to homeschool, no one in my circle had ever done it. I felt hidden, unsure, and out of place—but I sensed God leading me, and I chose to trust Him, one small obedient step at a time.

Sometimes we feel tucked away, hidden, or forgotten. But the same God who saw Esther sees you. The process of being hidden is often the first step in being crowned. Before a queen is revealed, she is refined.

In Esther 2, we see that the process of becoming royal didn't begin with the crown on her head—it began with being brought into the palace, into preparation. Even then, she didn't fight for attention. The Word says she simply pleased the one in charge. Her beauty, her grace, and her spirit set her apart.

SKINCARE RHYTHM

Gentle Cleanse

Tonight, as you begin your skincare routine, pause and let the warm water represent the beginning of a deeper cleansing—not just of your skin, but of your spirit. As you gently cleanse your face, reflect on what needs to be washed away—lies, comparison, unworthiness, shame. Let this moment be soft, intentional, and sacred. Apply cleanser and gently massage into face and around eye area, rinse off and dry with soft cloth, use am/pm. Double cleansing with Anointed Cleansing Oil & Crowned Glow Foam Cleanser is recommended.

Declaration:
I am chosen. I am seen.

ESTABLISHING RHYTHMS

JOURNAL REFLECTIONS

Start by reflecting honestly on your current lifestyle.
Sit with God and ask:

"What part of me needs more tending to right now?"
"Where am I not living well?"

"What's one area You want to restore?"

Then write down 3 intentional action steps to care for yourself in the area He's highlighting.

DATE

DAILY JOURNAL
YOUR THOUGHTS

AREA GOD IS HIGHLIGHTING

ACTION STEPS

WEEK 2

THE PROCESS OF PREPARATION

THEME:
PREPARATION ISN'T PUNISHMENT—IT'S PURPOSE.

SCRIPTURE:
"BEFORE A YOUNG WOMAN'S TURN CAME TO GO IN TO KING XERXES, SHE HAD TO COMPLETE TWELVE MONTHS OF BEAUTY TREATMENTS PRESCRIBED FOR THE WOMEN—SIX MONTHS WITH OIL OF MYRRH AND SIX WITH PERFUMES AND COSMETICS."
— ESTHER 2:12 (NIV)

PRAYER:
LORD, EXFOLIATE THE LAYERS OF DOUBT AND FEAR FROM MY LIFE. STRIP AWAY THE RESIDUE OF PAST PAIN, FALSE BELIEFS, AND ANYTHING THAT KEEPS ME FROM STEPPING INTO THE WOMAN YOU CREATED ME TO BE. I SURRENDER TO YOUR PROCESS—EVEN WHEN IT FEELS SLOW OR UNSEEN—TRUSTING THAT YOU ARE PREPARING ME FOR SOMETHING GREATER. IN JESUS' NAME, AMEN.

DEVOTIONAL REFLECTION:

Esther didn't wake up one day and step into her royal purpose. She endured twelve months of preparation—carefully timed, intentional, and, perhaps, at times uncomfortable. The oils and perfumes weren't just about fragrance; they were part of a process that required patience, waiting, and transformation from the inside out.

What if your current season of discomfort is actually divine exfoliation? What if the very things that feel like delay are God's tools for renewal?

I remember feeling stretched and unseen in a season when I was pouring into everyone else but wondering if God was still working on me. Looking back, I see now that He was doing a deep work beneath the surface—removing old fears and revealing something new.

Spiritually, God invites us into a similar process—one of letting go, surrendering old mindsets, beliefs, and habits that no longer serve His purpose for us.

Just as Esther had to be prepared for her royal appointment, so must we allow God to prepare us for the places He's calling us into. It's not punishment—it's positioning.

Think of Moses in the desert for 40 years (Exodus 3–4). Think of David tending sheep long before he sat on the throne (1 Samuel 16). Even Jesus Himself went through a time of preparation in the wilderness (Matthew 4:1–11) before beginning His public ministry.

Preparation seasons can feel hidden, but they're holy. They are the spaces where God removes any doubt, polishes identity, and infuses us with strength and clarity.

SKINCARE RHYTHM

Cell Renewal

Exfoliation is such a fitting metaphor here. In skincare, exfoliation removes the buildup of dead skin cells so that new, radiant skin can emerge. As you use your Holy Glow Face Serum, your skin is being renewed. Infused with oils like frankincense and myrrh, to gently regenerate your cells.

Declaration:
I choose to live surrendered. I am being prepared, I am being renewed.

SHEDDING THE OLD

JOURNAL REFLECTIONS

What old mindsets do I need to shed?

How can I welcome God's preparation process with grace?

How can I slow down and be present in the process?

Scriptures for Deeper Meditation:
Use the R.E.I.G.N method
Romans 12:2
Isaiah 43:18-19
2 Corinthians 4:16

DATE

DAILY JOURNAL
YOUR THOUGHTS

AREA GOD IS HIGHLIGHTING | ACTION STEPS

TRANSFORMATION HAPPENS IN STILLNESS

WEEK 3

BEAUTY TREATMENTS & BECOMING

THEME:
TRANSFORMATION HAPPENS IN STILLNESS.

SCRIPTURE:
"AND WHEN THE TURN CAME FOR EACH YOUNG WOMAN TO GO IN TO KING XERXES AFTER THE TWELVE MONTHS UNDER THE REGULATIONS FOR THE WOMEN, SINCE THIS WAS THE REGULAR PERIOD OF THEIR BEAUTIFYING... THEN THE YOUNG WOMAN WENT IN TO THE KING IN THIS WAY..."
— ESTHER 2:12-13 (ESV)

PRAYER:
GOD, NOURISH ME IN THE SECRET PLACE. I GIVE YOU PERMISSION TO WORK BENEATH THE SURFACE, TO TOUCH THE TENDER PLACES OF MY SOUL THAT NEED HEALING. HELP ME TO REST IN THE STILLNESS OF YOUR LOVE. THANK YOU FOR BEING A GENTLE FATHER. IN JESUS' NAME, AMEN.

DEVOTIONAL REFLECTION:

Esther's journey to the palace was not only external—it was deeply internal. After months of beauty treatments, her moment came. But what we often overlook is the stillness, the surrender, and the sacred work that took place beneath the surface.

Stillness is a powerful spiritual practice. It is in the quiet where God often does His most profound work. Psalm 46:10 says, "Be still and know that I am God." Becoming who He's called you to be isn't about striving—it's about surrendering to the gentle rhythms of grace.

I've had to learn this in my own life—especially in seasons where I wanted to do more, but God was asking me to be still. It was in the quiet of the night, after my children had gone to bed, that He would gently meet me—reminding me that even in the stillness, I was becoming.

Just like Esther trusted the process, we are invited to trust God with what lies beneath the surface. He's not intimidated by what you've been hiding. In fact, He longs to meet you there—to soothe, to cleanse, to restore.

And beauty? It's more than skin deep. True beauty, in the Kingdom, is found in a heart fully yielded to the King. "Your beauty should not come from outward adornment… rather, it should be that of your inner self, the unfading beauty of a gentle and quiet spirit" (1 Peter 3:3–4).

SKINCARE RHYTHM

Facial Treatment

Facials are more than indulgence. They're about softening, cleansing, and restoring—often with the help of a skilled hand. Sometimes we need someone to hold space for us, just like Esther had maids assigned to her (Esther 2:9). You weren't created to go through your transformation alone. This week, let your esthetician hold your face, let her be the hands of Jesus. Let Jesus breathe into you. Let the layers melt away in the quiet place.

Declaration:

I am worthy. I am loved. I am held.

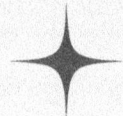

JOURNAL REFLECTIONS

What is God revealing in the quiet moments of self-care?

How do I define beauty through a Kingdom lens?

How open am I to receiving and allowing others to support me in this process?

Scriptures for Deeper Meditation:
Use the R.E.I.G.N method

1 Peter 3:3-4

Psalm 46:10

Isaiah 30:15

Matthew 11:28-29

DATE

DAILY JOURNAL
YOUR THOUGHTS

_____

_____

_____

_____

_____

_____

_____

AREA GOD IS HIGHLIGHTING	ACTION STEPS

YOUR UNIQUE GLOW ATTRACTS FAVOR

WEEK 4

FAVOR IN THE PALACE

THEME:
YOUR UNIQUE GLOW ATTRACTS DIVINE FAVOR.

SCRIPTURE:
"WHEN THE TURN CAME FOR ESTHER... SHE WON THE FAVOR OF EVERYONE WHO SAW HER... AND THE KING WAS ATTRACTED TO ESTHER MORE THAN TO ANY OF THE OTHER WOMEN... SO HE SET A ROYAL CROWN ON HER HEAD AND MADE HER QUEEN."
— ESTHER 2:15-17 (NIV)

PRAYER:
FATHER, ALIGN ME WITH THE FAVOR MEANT FOR ME. HELP ME TO WALK IN QUIET CONFIDENCE, TRUSTING THAT WHAT YOU'VE ANOINTED ME FOR CANNOT BE TAKEN BY ANYONE ELSE. LET MY LIFE REFLECT YOUR GRACE, YOUR BEAUTY, AND YOUR BALANCE. THANK YOU FOR THE DOORS YOU'VE ALREADY OPENED—AND THE ONES STILL WAITING. IN JESUS' NAME, AMEN.

DEVOTIONAL REFLECTION:

Esther carried something she didn't strive for—it was favor.

She didn't manipulate her way into position; she simply walked into what had already been prepared for her. She wasn't flashy or forceful, yet something about her drew others in.

Notice what Esther did in verse 15: "she asked for nothing except what Hegai, the king's eunuch who was in charge of the harem, suggested." This was a woman who knew how to yield. Her glow came not just from treatments, but from wisdom, humility, and God's hand.

For years, I operated my business through the lens of hustle culture—constantly pushing, performing, and trying to prove my worth. But God began to gently lead me out of that cycle and into a place of rest and abiding in Him. It was there, in that surrendered space, that I began to experience true favor—open doors I didn't have to force and opportunities aligned with His timing, not mine.

Favor doesn't require you to be loud or known—it requires you to be faithful. And when God places favor on your life, it's unmistakable. Like David, who was anointed king while still tending sheep (1 Samuel 16:11–13), or Ruth, who found favor in Boaz's eyes simply by gleaning faithfully in the field (Ruth 2:10), favor finds those aligned with God's heart.

SKINCARE RHYTHM

Toning

In skincare, toning restores balance and prepares the skin to receive what comes next. Spiritually, divine favor works much the same way—it brings alignment, opening doors that no man can shut (Revelation 3:8). It's not earned through effort, but received through alignment with God's purpose. As you spray your Royal Beauty Essence, receive the favor and carry it with you. Use toner after cleansing the skin am/pm.

Declaration:
I am favored. I am aligned with my Father's will.

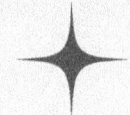

JOURNAL REFLECTIONS

Where have I experienced God's favor unexpectedly?
How can I walk in that favor boldly this week?

Scriptures for Deeper Meditation:
Use the R.E.I.G.N method

Proverbs 3:3-4

Psalm 90:17

Revelation 3:8

Ruth 2:10

DATE

DAILY JOURNAL
YOUR THOUGHTS

AREA GOD IS HIGHLIGHTING

ACTION STEPS

WEEK 5

THE POWER OF IDENTITY

THEME:
SOMETIMES WISDOM MEANS WAITING.

SCRIPTURE:
"BUT ESTHER HAD KEPT SECRET HER FAMILY BACKGROUND AND NATIONALITY JUST AS MORDECAI HAD TOLD HER TO DO, FOR SHE CONTINUED TO FOLLOW MORDECAI'S INSTRUCTIONS AS SHE HAD DONE WHEN HE WAS BRINGING HER UP."
— ESTHER 2:20 (NIV)

PRAYER:
GOD, REMIND ME OF WHO I AM IN YOU. IN A WORLD THAT TRIES TO LABEL AND DEFINE ME, HELP ME STAY ROOTED IN YOUR TRUTH. HEAL THE HIDDEN PLACES THAT I'VE COVERED IN FEAR OR SHAME. LET YOUR WORD BE THE SERUM THAT SINKS DEEP AND RESTORES MY TRUE IDENTITY. MAY I WALK WITH THE QUIET CONFIDENCE OF A DAUGHTER WHO KNOWS SHE'S DEEPLY KNOWN AND DIVINELY CHOSEN. IN JESUS' NAME, AMEN.

DEVOTIONAL REFLECTION:

Esther's identity—her heritage, her roots—remained hidden not out of shame, but out of wisdom. There is a sacredness to knowing who you are, even when you're not fully known by others.

God often forms identity in the quiet. In the unseen. Like Jesus growing in wisdom and stature before His ministry began (Luke 2:52), or Joseph learning humility in a prison before ruling in a palace (Genesis 41:14–40). These were seasons of being hidden—but not forgotten.

I remember a time in my life when I felt completely unseen—mothering, building, and healing in private. But it was in that hidden season that God reintroduced me to who I truly was—not based on what I did, but in who He created me to be.

Esther's obedience to Mordecai reveals a woman grounded in her upbringing, yet led by wisdom. She didn't need to prove who she was; she waited for the right moment to be revealed. This is the power of identity rooted in God—you're not swayed by recognition, because you're anchored in who He says you are.

This week, let God speak into your hidden places. Ask Him to reveal what needs to be healed, remembered, or reclaimed. Your identity is not what the world says—it's what God has declared over you from the beginning.

SKINCARE RHYTHM

Serums

Serums in skincare are deeply concentrated—they are the most intentional part of your routine. They're designed to target specific concerns and reveal radiant results over time. They're not for instant glow, but for lasting transformation.

This mirrors the kind of identity work God calls us to. It's deep, intentional, and requires trust in His timing. Use your Royal Beauty Serum to nourish your skin and allow God to nourish your soul. Use after toner am/pm.

Declaration:

I am radiant. I am a daughter of the King. I am infused and filled with my Father's love.

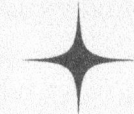

JOURNAL REFLECTIONS

What parts of my identity do I still keep hidden?

What has God called me, even when I forget?

Scriptures for Deeper Meditation:
Use the R.E.I.G.N method

Isaiah 43:1

Luke 2:52

Colossians 3:3

DATE

DAILY JOURNAL
YOUR THOUGHTS

AREA GOD IS HIGHLIGHTING | ACTION STEPS

FOR SUCH A TIME AS THIS

WEEK 6

COURAGE IN THE CALL

THEME:
YOU WERE BORN FOR SUCH A TIME AS THIS.

SCRIPTURE:
"DO NOT THINK THAT BECAUSE YOU ARE IN THE KING'S HOUSE YOU ALONE OF ALL THE JEWS WILL ESCAPE. FOR IF YOU REMAIN SILENT AT THIS TIME, RELIEF AND DELIVERANCE FOR THE JEWS WILL ARISE FROM ANOTHER PLACE... AND WHO KNOWS BUT THAT YOU HAVE COME TO YOUR ROYAL POSITION FOR SUCH A TIME AS THIS?" — ESTHER 4:13–14

PRAYER:
GIVE ME BOLDNESS, LORD, TO STEP INTO THE CALL ON MY LIFE. STIR THE PLACES WITHIN ME THAT HAVE GROWN QUIET OR AFRAID. REMIND ME THAT I AM NOT ALONE—YOU GO BEFORE ME, AND YOU'VE ANOINTED ME FOR THIS MOMENT. JUST LIKE ESTHER, HELP ME RISE WITH QUIET COURAGE, TRUSTING THAT YOU'VE PLACED ME HERE, NOW, FOR DIVINE PURPOSE. I SAY YES, EVEN WHEN I'M TREMBLING.
IN JESUS' NAME, AMEN.

DEVOTIONAL REFLECTION:

Like facial massage awakens what's beneath the surface, the Spirit of God is awakening your courage. It's already there—He's simply stirring it.

That's what Mordecai was doing for Esther—pressing gently but firmly on the places she might've felt afraid or stuck, calling her courage to the surface.

Esther's moment of calling wasn't loud. It was sacred. There was no parade, no clear voice from the sky—just a nudge, a conversation, and a choice. She could have remained silent, comfortable, even safe. But calling isn't always convenient. It stretches us beyond comfort and into kingdom impact.

A few years ago, God asked me to close my business—something that felt confusing and costly at the time. But that "yes" became the doorway to not just rebuilding my life, but co-creating something far greater: not just a brand, but a Spirit-led movement.

God is faithful to place us where we need to be, when we need to be there. But He also invites us to partner with Him. Esther's courage activated the flow of deliverance for a nation. What if your "yes" carries a breakthrough for someone else?

SKINCARE RHYTHM

Facial Massage

Facial massage does more than smooth the surface—it activates deeper circulation. It brings blood flow to stagnant areas, releases built-up tension, and awakens the skin to its natural glow. It's about encouraging what already lives within to rise and radiate. Facial massage can be done with hands or a tool like gua-sha or face roller. Can be done daily, recommended at least twice per week.

Declaration:

I have a good Father. Jesus, your glory overflows. Holy Spirit, you are present. I was born for such a time as this.

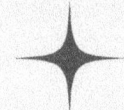

JOURNAL REFLECTIONS

What call is stirring in my heart?

What fears do I need to release in order to say yes?

Scriptures for Deeper Meditation:

Use the R.E.I.G.N method

2 Timothy 1:7

Isaiah 6:8

Joshua 1:9

Romans 8:30

DATE

DAILY JOURNAL
YOUR THOUGHTS

AREA GOD IS HIGHLIGHTING

ACTION STEPS

PREPARATION CONTINUES IN SURRENDER

WEEK 7

STEPPING OUT IN FAITH

THEME:
PREPARATION CONTINUES WITH SURRENDER.

SCRIPTURE:
"THEN ESTHER SENT THIS REPLY TO MORDECAI: 'GO, GATHER TOGETHER ALL THE JEWS WHO ARE IN SUSA, AND FAST FOR ME. DO NOT EAT OR DRINK FOR THREE DAYS, NIGHT OR DAY. I AND MY ATTENDANTS WILL FAST AS YOU DO. WHEN THIS IS DONE, I WILL GO TO THE KING, EVEN THOUGH IT IS AGAINST THE LAW. AND IF I PERISH, I PERISH.'"
— ESTHER 4:15–17 (NIV)

PRAYER:
I RELEASE THE THINGS I'VE HELD ONTO TOO TIGHTLY—CONTROL, FEAR, DISTRACTIONS, DOUBT. CREATE SPACE WITHIN ME TO HEAR YOUR VOICE MORE CLEARLY. I TRUST THAT WHAT YOU HAVE AHEAD IS GREATER THAN WHAT I LEAVE BEHIND. LET THIS ACT OF SURRENDER BE AN OFFERING. PURIFY MY HEART. ALIGN MY SPIRIT. PREPARE ME NOT BY STRIVING, BUT BY TRUSTING.
IN JESUS' NAME, AMEN.

DEVOTIONAL REFLECTION:

Fasting is a detox of the soul. It creates space to hear God clearly by turning down the volume of the world. It is an act of release and trust, a declaration that His presence is more nourishing than anything we could consume.

I remember a season where the Lord asked me to fast—not just from food, but from distractions that I thought were necessary for success. Laying those things down felt like a loss at first, but it opened my ears and my heart in a way I hadn't experienced before.

Esther didn't go alone—she asked for a community to fast with her. Together, they leaned into the power of surrender.

When you fast—whether from food, distractions, or fear—you're stepping into faith. You're making room for clarity. For courage. For miracles.

As you detox this week, imagine every layer drawing out fear, doubt, comparison, or control. It's okay to see your skin purge what is necessary. Let the Lord speak in the stillness. Let your faith rise as you release.

Sometimes the most powerful preparation is surrender.

SKINCARE RHYTHM

Detox

The invitation in your skincare routine here is not to do more, but rather to slow down. Observe what your skin is showing you. Before you start your skincare routine, take 3 deep breaths. This will level up your routine. Practice incorporating this daily into your nighttime routine to help you unwind and have better sleep.

Declaration:

I am moving at the pace of grace. I inhale God's goodness and release any toxic beliefs about myself.

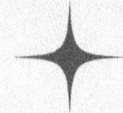

JOURNAL REFLECTIONS

What do I need to fast from this week to hear God clearly?
What breakthrough am I believing for?
What am I making room for?

Scriptures for Deeper Meditation:
Use the R.E.I.G.N method

Joel 2:12

Isaiah 58:6

Matthew 6:17-18

Psalm 46:10

DATE

✶ DAILY JOURNAL
YOUR THOUGHTS

_____

_____

_____

_____

_____

_____

_____

AREA GOD IS HIGHLIGHTING	ACTION STEPS

WEEK 8

APPROACHING THE KING

THEME:
BOLDNESS IN IDENTITY BRINGS ACCESS.

SCRIPTURE:
"ON THE THIRD DAY ESTHER PUT ON HER ROYAL ROBES AND STOOD IN THE INNER COURT OF THE PALACE, IN FRONT OF THE KING'S HALL . . . WHEN HE SAW QUEEN ESTHER STANDING IN THE COURT, HE WAS PLEASED WITH HER AND HELD OUT TO HER THE GOLD SCEPTER... SO ESTHER APPROACHED AND TOUCHED THE TIP OF THE SCEPTER." — ESTHER 5:1-2

PRAYER:
FATHER, I COME TO YOU THIRSTY FOR MORE OF YOUR PRESENCE. HYDRATE ME AT THE DEEPEST LEVEL—BODY, SPIRIT, AND SOUL. LET YOUR LIVING WATER REFRESH MY IDENTITY AND RESTORE MY BOLDNESS.
I RECEIVE THE FAVOR THAT FLOWS FROM YOU ALONE, AND I WALK INTO THIS WEEK CONFIDENT, HYDRATED, AND WHOLE.
IN JESUS' NAME, AMEN.

DEVOTIONAL REFLECTION:

Esther stepped into the king's court clothed in royal robes—but her confidence came from something far deeper than fabric. She had been nourished and prepared, and now she was ready to approach with boldness.

True hydration goes beyond surface-level care. It begins within—cell by cell, drop by drop—just like boldness begins not in appearance but in identity and intimacy with the King.

John 4:14 reminds us of a deeper thirst: "Whoever drinks the water I give them will never thirst. Indeed, the water I give them will become in them a spring of water welling up to eternal life."

When we nourish our bodies with pure, living water, we activate restoration and vitality at the cellular level. But when we nourish our spirit with the Living Water of Jesus, we access the deep well of confidence that never runs dry.

I remember walking through a season where I was doing all the right things—skincare, wellness routines, prayer—but still felt dry and depleted. I was struggling with a health condition, and no matter what I tried, healing felt out of reach. It wasn't until God opened my eyes to the toxic environments I was staying in, places draining my spirit, that I realized I was being stripped dry. I realized I needed to have awareness of what was happening. Only then was I able to seek strength and confidence from Him to walk away because of who I am in Him, finally allowing me to be filled by His living water.

Esther didn't just look royal—she moved from a place of knowing **whose** she was. And because of that, the King extended favor.

You are invited into the same holy access.

SKINCARE RHYTHM

Skin Hydration

Water is one of the most overlooked nutrient especially when it comes to your skin. Drinking not just enough water but water that truly hydrates at the cellular level ensures all of your organs are functioning optimally, including your skin (your largest organ). Implement more hydration with ionized, hydrogen water.

Declaration:

I am a well filled with living water. God you are my primary source to living in wholeness.

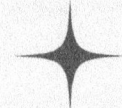

JOURNAL REFLECTIONS

What does it look like for me to confidently approach God today?

Where do I need to walk with queenly confidence this week?

Scriptures for Deeper Meditation:
Use the R.E.I.G.N method

John 4:14

Hebrews 4:16

Isaiah 55:1

DATE

DAILY JOURNAL
YOUR THOUGHTS

AREA GOD IS HIGHLIGHTING

ACTION STEPS

QUEENS MOVE
WITH WISDOM
AND TIMING

WEEK 9

STRATEGY & DISCERNMENT

THEME:

QUEENS MOVE WITH WISDOM AND TIMING.

SCRIPTURE:

"THEN THE KING ASKED, 'WHAT IS IT, QUEEN ESTHER? WHAT IS YOUR REQUEST? EVEN UP TO HALF THE KINGDOM, IT WILL BE GIVEN YOU.' 'IF IT PLEASES THE KING,' REPLIED ESTHER, 'LET THE KING, TOGETHER WITH HAMAN, COME TO A BANQUET I HAVE PREPARED…'" — ESTHER 5:3-8

PRAYER:

LORD, GIVE ME EYES THAT SEE WITH WISDOM AND CLARITY. ANOINT MY VISION TO RECOGNIZE YOUR TIMING AND STRATEGY.

TEACH ME TO MOVE WITH PRECISION, LIKE ESTHER, TO WAIT WHEN YOU SAY WAIT AND SPEAK WHEN YOU SAY SPEAK.

MAY MY GAZE BE FIXED ON YOU, AND MAY YOUR DISCERNMENT SHINE THROUGH ME.

IN JESUS' NAME, AMEN.

DEVOTIONAL REFLECTION:

Esther didn't rush. She could have made her request the moment she stepped into the king's presence—but instead, she waited. She discerned the moment, prepared a table, and moved with wisdom, grace, and precision.

This is the power of strategy, born in stillness and prayer.

I've learned this in my own journey—especially when I felt pressured to "do it all" in my business and life. It took stepping back, pausing in prayer, and trusting God's timing before making big decisions. That stillness brought clarity I couldn't find in the rush.

Just like the delicate area under your eyes needs intentional care to stay bright and youthful, your spiritual vision needs covering and clarity. Using eye cream reminds us to pause and see with intention—to unveil what God is doing behind the scenes and discern what He's calling us to do next.

James 1:5 says, "If any of you lacks wisdom, you should ask God, who gives generously to all without finding fault." God is not withholding direction—He's inviting you to slow down long enough to receive it.

Esther teaches us that wisdom is not just about knowing what to do—but also when and how to do it. It's a radiant gaze—sharp, discerning, and full of grace.

SKINCARE RHYTHM

Eye Cream

Unveiling clarity, seeing with divine discernment. Gently apply eye cream under your eye area and tap it into the skin. Use Radiant Gaze Eye Cream am/pm after serum.

Declaration:

God, I trust your timing. I receive your wisdom to see clearly. I am unveiled, I am wise.

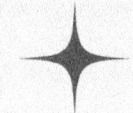

JOURNAL REFLECTIONS

Where is God asking me to wait on His timing?

What strategy has He already placed in my heart?

Scriptures for Deeper Meditation:
Use the R.E.I.G.N method

James 1:5
Proverbs 3:5-6
Isaiah 30:21

DATE

DAILY JOURNAL
YOUR THOUGHTS

AREA GOD IS HIGHLIGHTING | ACTION STEPS

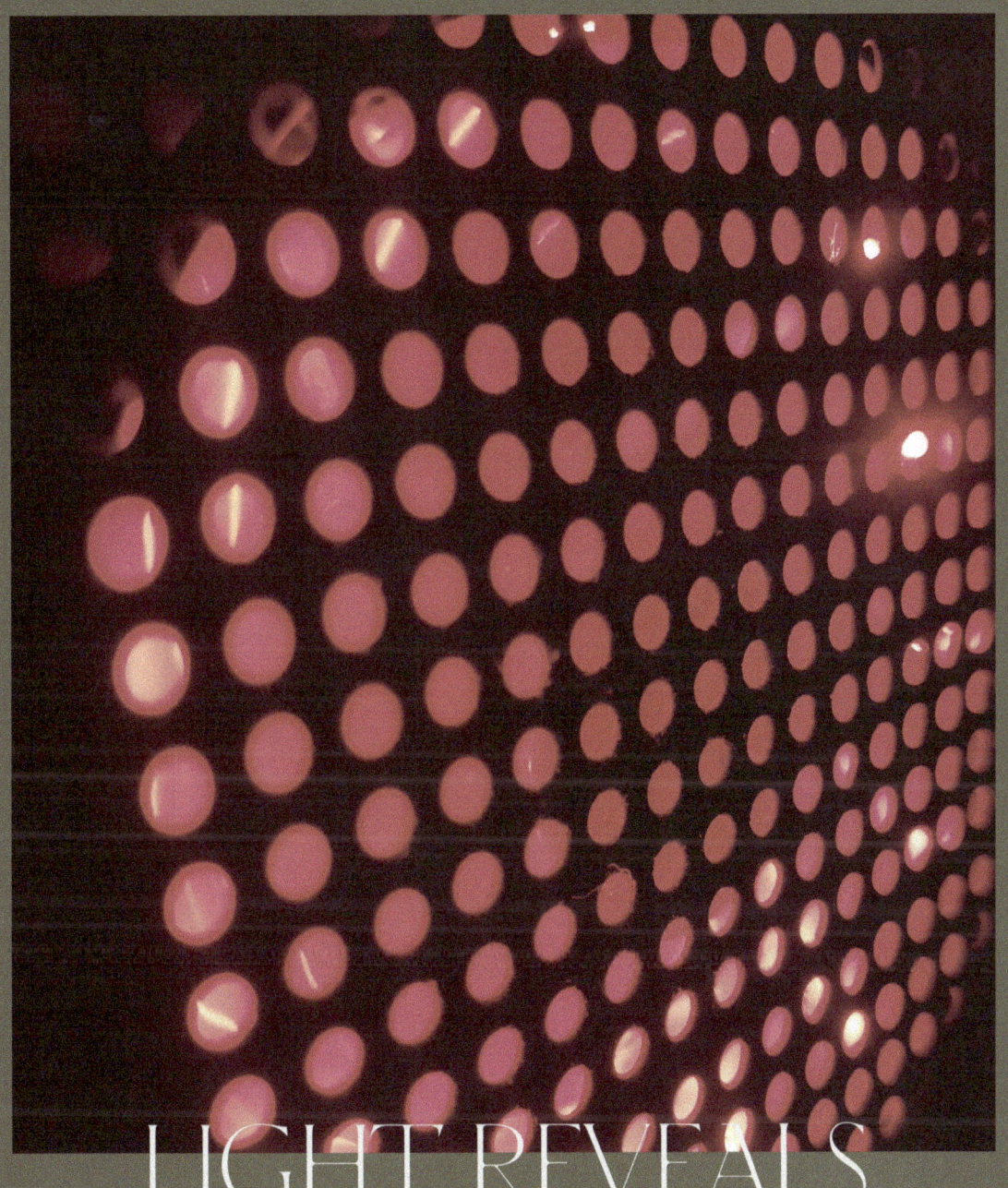

LIGHT REVEALS WHAT MUST BE HEALED

WEEK 10

EXPOSING THE ENEMY

THEME:
LIGHT REVEALS WHAT MUST BE HEALED OR REMOVED.

SCRIPTURE:
"THEN QUEEN ESTHER ANSWERED, 'IF I HAVE FOUND FAVOR WITH YOU, YOUR MAJESTY . . . LET MY LIFE BE GIVEN ME—THAT IS MY PETITION. AND THE LIVES OF MY PEOPLE… BECAUSE WE HAVE BEEN SOLD TO BE DESTROYED . . .'"
— ESTHER 7:1-6 (NIV)

PRAYER:
LORD, EXPOSE WHAT I CAN'T SEE.
SHINE YOUR LIGHT ON EVERY LIE, EVERY ROOT OF FEAR, EVERY HIDDEN STRONGHOLD IN MY HEART.
REVEAL WHAT MUST BE HEALED. REMOVE WHAT DOESN'T REFLECT YOU.
LIKE ESTHER, GIVE ME THE BOLDNESS TO SPEAK TRUTH WITH LOVE AND THE CLARITY TO SEE THE REAL BATTLE.
I SURRENDER TO THE LIGHT OF YOUR HEALING PRESENCE.
IN JESUS' NAME, AMEN.

DEVOTIONAL REFLECTION:

Up until this point, Esther has been quiet, discerning, and preparing. But now—it's time to expose. There are times in our own healing when God gently brings to light hidden wounds we didn't realize were still lingering—deep-rooted beliefs, fears, and spiritual battles. For me, growing up without my dad in my life left a quiet ache I didn't always recognize. It shaped how I saw myself—sometimes feeling unworthy, unseen, or not enough—and it influenced the kind of relationships I allowed myself to have, often settling for less than I deserved or struggling to fully trust.

This process of uncovering those wounds wasn't about shame—it was about freedom. It was painful to face how those early experiences shaped my heart, but it was necessary. Ephesians 5:13 reminds us, "Everything exposed by the light becomes visible—and everything that is illuminated becomes a light." What the enemy tried to keep hidden in darkness, God is ready to heal and redeem for His glory.

Just like Esther didn't hold back when her moment came, we are invited to name the things that have tried to silence us. There is power and healing in bringing those shadows into the light and surrendering them to Christ's love.

SKINCARE RHYTHM

Red Light Therapy

Just like red light therapy targets what's beneath the surface—acne, inflammation, and aging. The light reveals it to be healed. Use light therapy daily before bedtime after your skincare routine for 10–15 minutes.

Declaration:

I am the light of the world. Jesus, as your light reveals areas of my heart that need healing, let the light reflect onto others, so we may all be whole.

JOURNAL REFLECTIONS

What spiritual or emotional enemies need to be confronted?

What strongholds are breaking in this season?

Scriptures for Deeper Meditation:
Use the R.E.I.G.N method

Ephesians 5:13
2 Corinthians 10:4
John 1:5
Psalm 139:23-24

DATE

✻
DAILY JOURNAL

AREA GOD IS HIGHLIGHTING | ACTION STEPS

GOD HAS MARKED YOU WITH HIS AUTHORITY

WEEK 11

SEALED WITH AUTHORITY

THEME:
GOD HAS MARKED YOU WITH HIS AUTHORITY—
AND HIS WORD NEVER RETURNS VOID.

SCRIPTURE:
"THAT SAME DAY KING XERXES GAVE QUEEN ESTHER THE ESTATE OF HAMAN... THE KING TOOK OFF HIS SIGNET RING, WHICH HE HAD RECLAIMED FROM HAMAN, AND PRESENTED IT TO MORDECAI... MORDECAI WROTE IN THE NAME OF KING XERXES, SEALED THE DISPATCHES WITH THE KING'S SIGNET RING, AND SENT THEM . . . "— ESTHER 8:1-17 (NIV-SELECT VERSES)

PRAYER:
FATHER, THANK YOU FOR SEALING ME WITH YOUR SPIRIT.
WHERE THERE WAS ONCE FEAR AND DEFEAT, YOU HAVE WRITTEN A NEW DECREE OVER MY LIFE.
LET EVERY STEP I TAKE BE ALIGNED WITH YOUR AUTHORITY.
I DECLARE THAT I AM SEALED, SECURED, AND SENT IN YOUR NAME.
MAY THE GLOW OF YOUR GOODNESS REST UPON ME, AND MAY I WALK IN THE FULLNESS OF YOUR FAVOR.
IN JESUS' NAME, AMEN.

DEVOTIONAL REFLECTION:

Esther's bravery shifted an entire nation's destiny—but her victory wasn't complete until it was sealed. The king gave Mordecai the signet ring—a symbol of royal authority—and what was written in the king's name could not be revoked. There was a moment when the weight of doubt and uncertainty finally lifted, and the truth of who I am in God flooded my heart. It was as if a veil was lifted, and I saw myself through His eyes—worthy, chosen, and powerful. From that place, my words began to carry new life; they shifted my mindset, changed my actions, and transformed the very atmosphere around me. The authority God gave me wasn't just a concept—it became my daily reality, breathing confidence and peace into every step I took.

Ephesians 1:13 says, "When you believed, you were marked in Him with a seal, the promised Holy Spirit." Just as the king's decree stood by the seal of the ring, your life stands secure in the authority of Heaven. Where the enemy once had influence, you now stand clothed in purpose, anointed with authority, and sealed by the Spirit. God has declared victory over your life—and no power of darkness can reverse it.

Like a rich, nourishing balm, let that truth settle deep into you today: You are sealed. You are secure. You are sent.

SKINCARE RHYTHM

Moisturizer

Sealing in the nourishment, locking in protection, and affirming identity—like being sealed by the Holy Spirit with divine authority. In skincare, moisturizer is the final sealing step. It locks in all the nourishing work that came before—protection, healing, and glow. Apply your Royal Beauty Cream in the morning, following your serum and Holy Glow Hydration Balm at night following your serum.

Declaration:

I am nourished, and I am sealed by the Holy Spirit. I walk with divine authority in Jesus.

JOURNAL REFLECTIONS

What battles has God already turned in my favor?

How can I walk in His authority this week with confidence?

Scriptures for Deeper Meditation:
Use the R.E.I.G.N method

Ephesians 1:13

2 Corinthians 1:21-22

Esther 8:8

DATE

DAILY JOURNAL
YOUR THOUGHTS

AREA GOD IS HIGHLIGHTING

ACTION STEPS

YOU WERE RESTORED TO REIGN

WEEK 12
RESTORED TO REIGN

THEME:
YOU WERE RESTORED TO REIGN—
AND YOUR GLOW IS MEANT TO OVERFLOW.

SCRIPTURE:
"SO QUEEN ESTHER DAUGHTER OF ABIHAIL, ALONG WITH MORDECAI THE JEW, WROTE WITH FULL AUTHORITY TO CONFIRM THIS SECOND LETTER... KING XERXES IMPOSED TRIBUTE... AND ALL HIS ACTS OF POWER AND MIGHT... ARE THEY NOT WRITTEN...? MORDECAI THE JEW WAS SECOND IN RANK... HELD IN HIGH ESTEEM... BECAUSE HE WORKED FOR THE GOOD OF HIS PEOPLE..."
— ESTHER 9:29–10:3 (NIV-SELECT VERSES)

PRAYER:
LORD, THANK YOU FOR RESTORING ME TO REIGN.
NOT IN PRIDE, BUT IN PURPOSE. NOT IN SELF-GLORY, BUT IN SURRENDERED GLOW. FILL ME AGAIN WITH YOUR SPIRIT—UNTIL IT OVERFLOWS. LET MY LIFE BE AN INVITATION FOR OTHERS TO COME AND TASTE THE FRUIT OF YOUR PRESENCE.
I RECEIVE MY CROWN WITH HUMILITY AND JOY, AND I CHOOSE TO WALK IN LOVE, WISDOM, AND RADIANT FAITH.
IN JESUS' NAME, AMEN.

DEVOTIONAL REFLECTION:

Esther's story didn't end at rescue—it ended in restoration and reigning. She didn't just survive the threat—she emerged stronger, wiser, and crowned with authority. Like Esther, my journey toward restoration began when I finally allowed myself to be honest about my feelings, thoughts, and beliefs. It was then that God extended a gentle invitation to reconnect with my whole being—body, spirit, and soul. In that sacred space, I realized He was not distant but deeply present within me, wanting to reveal parts of myself that didn't align with who I truly am. This was the start of my restoration.

Esther stepped into her God-given role as queen not only for herself but for the good of her people. And that's what happens when you've been restored by the King—you reign with purpose. When filled with the Holy Spirit, His presence becomes like fruit—ripe, nourishing, and available for others to "taste and see that the Lord is good" (Psalm 34:8). Galatians 5:22-23 reminds us that the fruit of the Spirit—love, joy, peace, patience, kindness, self-control, faithfulness, gentleness, and goodness—are the evidence of a heart filled and sealed. Your glow ~~is not just aesthetic~~—it's spiritual. It's how others encounter Jesus through your peace, your strength, your stillness, your story.

You are restored not just to be radiant, but to reign in love, wisdom, and divine purpose.

SKINCARE RHYTHM

Crowned

Sealing in the glow, embracing your royal beauty, and preparing to pour out from a place of overflow is this week's skincare focus. This isn't just about looking radiant, but remaining intentional. It's about recognizing that the glow you carry is a reflection of what God has done in you. It's not just for you to enjoy. It's meant to overflow.

Declaration:

I am glowing, I am Royal beauty, I overflow God's beauty. I am the frangrance of Jesus. I am bold and confident in who God has made me to be.

JOURNAL REFLECTIONS

In what areas of my life has God restored me to reign?

How can I let the glow of His presence overflow into the lives of others?

Scriptures for Deeper Meditation:
Use the R.E.I.G.N method

Psalm 34:8

Galatians 5:22-23

1 Peter 2:9

Isaiah 61:3

DATE

DAILY JOURNAL
YOUR THOUGHTS

AREA GOD IS HIGHLIGHTING | ACTION STEPS

ABOUT MELISSA

HI, I'M MELISSA!

I'M A HOMESCHOOL MOM OF 3, LICENSED ESTHETICIAN WITH 12YRS+ IN THE INDUSTRY, AND THE FOUNDER OF EMBRACING ROYAL BEAUTY.

I'M PASSIONATE ABOUT EMPOWERING WOMEN TO LIVE WHOLE AND RADIANT LIVES, BLENDING MY LOVE FOR SKINCARE, WELLNESS, AND SPIRITUAL GROWTH. THROUGH MY WORK, I GUIDE WOMEN ON A JOURNEY OF SELF-CARE THAT NURTURES BOTH THE BODY AND SOUL, WITH A FOCUS ON LIVING AUTHENTICALLY IN GOD'S PURPOSE. I BELIEVE THAT BEAUTY IS A REFLECTION OF INNER WELLNESS, AND I'M HERE TO HELP YOU GLOW FROM THE INSIDE OUT—BODY, SOUL, AND SPIRIT.

GET CONNECTED

AT EMBRACING ROYAL BEAUTY, WE BELIEVE THAT HEALING, GROWTH, AND TRANSFORMATION FLOURISH IN COMMUNITY.

💌 JOIN OUR EMAIL LIST
BE THE FIRST TO RECEIVE HOLY GLOW DIARIES, EXCLUSIVE WELLNESS RESOURCES, EVENT INVITES, AND SKINCARE UPDATES.

BECOME A MEMBER
OUR MEMBERSHIP OFFERS DEEPER ACCESS TO HOLY GLOW RESOURCES, MONTHLY WELLNESS EVENTS, EXCLUSIVE PRODUCT DISCOUNTS, AND A SUPPORTIVE SISTERHOOD.

BOOK A SACRED FACIAL EXPERIENCE

SHOP OUR SKINCARE PRODUCTS

ATTEND A RETREAT OR EVENT
NEED A RESET? OUR HOLY GLOW RETREATS AND COLLECTIVE EVENTS OFFER IN-PERSON CONNECTION, RESTORATION, AND REVELATION.

VISIT, SHOP, BOOK & SUBSCRIBE:
EMBRACINGROYALBEAUTY.COM

📱 FOLLOW US ON INSTAGRAM
@EMBRACINGROYALBEAUTY